THEN & NOW

PERTH AMBOY

Opposite: Here is a typical Perth Amboy sidewalk scene on Washington Street during the blizzard of 1888, showing frozen wires, impassible snowdrifts, and bewildered citizens looking on in the storm. During the blizzard, helpful policemen rubbed the noses and ears of pedestrians with snow to restore circulation. (Courtesy of the Perth Amboy Public Library.)

THEN & NOW

PERTH AMBOY

Paul W. Wang and
Katherine A. Massopust

For my brother, Dale whose love of history and of Perth Amboy inspired me to write this book. For my mother, Catherine Merritt-Wang and my best friend Jack M. Dudas, Esq.
—Paul

For my grandmother, Anne Zaleski.
—Katherine

Copyright © 2009 by Paul W. Wang and Katherine A. Massopust
ISBN 978-0-7385-6241-4

Library of Congress Control Number: 2008934221

Published by Arcadia Publishing
Charleston SC, Chicago IL, Portsmouth NH, San Francisco CA

Printed in the United States of America

For all general information contact Arcadia Publishing at:
Telephone 843-853-2070
Fax 843-853-0044
E-mail sales@arcadiapublishing.com
For customer service and orders:
Toll-Free 1-888-313-2665

Visit us on the Internet at www.arcadiapublishing.com

On the front cover: Pictured are aerial shots of Smith Street in the 1920s and during the Perth Amboy Waterfront Festival in 2005. (Historic image courtesy of Jack M. Dudas Esq. and Barbara Booz; modern image, courtesy of Paul W. Wang.)

On the back cover: Please see page 72 for more information. (Courtesy of Jack M. Dudas Esq. and Barbara Booz.)

CONTENTS

ACKNOWLEDGMENTS

No one person could build a city like Perth Amboy, and no one person could create a book like this.

We wish to give special thanks to William Pavlovsky, former city historian of Perth Amboy, for his insight and personal knowledge of Perth Amboy's history and its architecture. We also wish to thank Jack M. Dudas Esq. for use of his personal collection of vintage photographs and his knowledge of Perth Amboy history. Thanks go to the staff of the Perth Amboy Public Library, including Patricia Gandy, Jessisca Zulin, Herschel Chomsky, Edwin Olavarria, Manuel Sanpof, Mary Bonilla, and William Baez for their helpfulness and collection of photographs that they allowed for use in this book. For their contribution to this book, we wish to thank the following: Barbara Booz, owner and proprietor of the Maid of Perth Collectibles store in Perth Amboy, for the use of some of her photographs; John Dyke of Dyke Insurance Company and his family for use of their personal collection of vintage photographs and for our many discussions of Perth Amboy's past; King High Garage and Autobody's owners, James Schreck, his son James Gougeon, and nephew Robert Chryssikos, for use of their vintage photograph; Dave Maldonado and family of Professional Automotives for the use of vintage photographs; Rick Fertig and his family for their photograph of Fertig's; and Paulo and Francis Sciortino and Lou Seminski Sr. for the photograph of Sciortino's. We also want to thank the following for their help with written information and their knowledge: Barbara Stack, former president of the Kearny Cottage Historical Association, who was very helpful with putting the puzzle together; James Hardiman for his insight on the history of the Seaman family; A. J. Massopust for his insight about the Perth Amboy Fire Department and the locations, dates, and times of fires; Joan Zaleski for providing past written materials; and Walter Hullfish for many hours of enjoyable talks and information about St. Mary's and Perth Amboy. We wish to thank author Paul W. Wang's sisters Faith Hernandez and Angel Wang for their support during this project. Also, a special thanks goes to the city of Perth Amboy, whose charm is timeless.

All contemporary images appearing here are courtesy of author Paul W. Wang.

INTRODUCTION

Paul W. Wang and his wife, Katherine Massopust, are both lifelong residents of Perth Amboy. Paul Wang has been a professional photographer for over 30 years and has personally witnessed many changes of Perth Amboy's dynamic community through the lens of his camera.

This book explores the diverse buildings of the city of Perth Amboy through both historic and contemporary images. It is hoped that readers will see not just words and pictures but also a glimpse into Perth Amboy's rich and diverse culture. It is a city with an important role in the founding of the United States of America. Perth Amboy was home to William Franklin, the last royal governor of New Jersey and son of Benjamin Franklin. It is where the Bill of Rights was first signed. The first African American voter, Thomas Mundy Peterson, resided here. Throughout its time, Perth Amboy was always a seaport, and its industry has always reflected this. The city has progressed from the oyster industry in the 1700s and 1800s to the industrial age, as Raritan Steel, Chevron Oil, and Hess Oil used the Raritan Bay as a means of transporting their goods. Perhaps the best way to see this glimpse of Perth Amboy's history is to look at each building described as not only a heap of mortar and brick but also as a living center of history of the city.

In the history of American, artists, and actors, Perth Amboy occupies a place of importance. John Watson, "the first American painter," lived in Perth Amboy. William Dunlap, author of *The Arts of Design in America*, was born here, lived here most of his life, and did much of his work here. Other great American artists who lived in Perth Amboy include George Inness, Victoria Ciani, Lindsay Morris Sterling, Louis Comfort Tiffany, and Francis Kearny, who was one of the greatest engravers of his time. Ruth White has gained fame as an actress and has made her native city known again in the theatrical world. Also, her brother Charles White was an actor that helped his native city to become known.

In the early days of its inception, the town was smaller but of great value. The edifices told of in this book were the focal points of early Perth Amboy and those who lived in and around them gave life to the future bay city. To have some knowledge of these structures is to begin to understand Perth Amboy. At one time, this city was known under different names, including Po Ambo, Amboy Point, Point Amboy, and Amboy. The story is that the Native American name of Amboy designated the high-level plain upon which the city was founded, surrounded on the east by the Raritan River. With the entrance of Lord Perth onto the board, the appellation of Perth was decided upon by the board of proprietors, and it was designated as Perth Town. The Amboy part could not be dropped so readily, and they were joined together into Perth Amboy.

The past is captured by the captions and photographs told in this book. Out of the past comes the present, exemplified by the busy streets of Perth Amboy, the downtown district, new schools, new homes, new stores, and new community facilities. Out of these present-day structures, an exciting future will emerge.

A newcomer to Perth Amboy can easily note that the city is one of contrasts. These contrasts grew out of the early life of Perth Amboy. The Smith Street or downtown area is visited daily by hundreds of shoppers and employees. Sadowski Parkway, named in honor of the late army sergeant Joseph Sadowski (posthumously awarded the Medal of Honor), offers a serene and quiet scene along the Perth Amboy waterfront. Two of Perth Amboy's heavily trafficked streets are Hall Avenue and State Street. These two streets offer a taste of Latin American life. Public housing projects offer a feeling of a heavily urban environment that is balanced by the one- and two-family homes in the western section of the city, which gives a feeling of suburban charm. There are over 40 different churches and synagogues in Perth Amboy, which is a perfect example of the town's ethnic diversity. Factories with humming machinery employ hundreds of individuals, while the schools of Perth Amboy, both public and parochial, educate future leaders.

The one thing constant about Perth Amboy is change. Some change is positive, some is negative, and some is a mixture of both, as shown through the images in this book. Over the years, Perth Amboy has experienced change in numerous ways. For example, the Majestic Theater building has seen many changes over the course of its time. Once a grand vaudeville theater in 1920s and 1930s, it became a major movie theater in the late 1930s through the mid-1960s. The building's last swan song as a theater was as an adult movie house, which lasted until the late 1970s. Now the building is the Second Baptist Church, also known as the Cathedral. It is heavily attended and has been totally remodeled. This is just one example of the many changes that occurred in the city. Even now, the mayor of 20 years Joseph Vas lost the election to Wilda Diaz, Perth Amboy's first female to hold the office.

As residents of Perth Amboy, the authors have enjoyed putting this book together for readers who enjoy history and photographs as much as they do. Whatever one's relationship to Perth Amboy may be, it is hoped that the past as reflected in these vintage images will speak to the reader in many ways. Perhaps these pages will awaken memories long forgotten; perhaps they will reveal a thread of unknown past history. But above all, it is hoped that life will be enriched and the sense of community strengthened by exploring the images in this book.

CHAPTER 1

TIMELESS AND CHANGING SMITH STREET

On July 4, 1932, Smith Street was bustling and filled with pedestrians celebrating Independence Day. Stores included Woolworths and S. S. Kresge's. There were many pool halls, including Beck Royal Pool Parlor and bars providing relaxation to the workingman. (Courtesy of Jack M. Dudas Esq.)

An aerial shot of Smith Street in the 1940s shows the bustling activity. Stores included S. S. Kresge's and Reynolds Department Store, which used the first pneumatic tubes for handling cash transactions. Stores may come and go on this busy street through the years, but Smith Street still remains as the heart of businesses located in Perth Amboy. Pictured in the contemporary image is the Perth Amboy Waterfront Festival in July 2006. (Historic image courtesy of Jack M. Dudas Esq. and Barbara Booz.)

TIMELESS AND CHANGING SMITH STREET

A typical scene from the late 1940s or early 1950s of State and Smith Streets shows a traffic officer, which is now replaced by a walk/do not walk sign. From this location one could go down to the waterfront or all the way to outer State Street. It is best known as "the five corners" because one can go in five different directions from this point in Perth Amboy. (Historic image courtesy of Jack M. Dudas Esq.)

Shown is upper Smith Street in the late 1930s or early 1940s, and to the right is the train station. Travelers coming to and from New York and the shore points often visited the many coffee shops and diners that served weary travelers, such as the Amboy Lunch and Costa's Hot Dog Stand. Costa's Hot Dog Stand is still serving visitors to this very day. (Historic image courtesy of Jack M. Dudas Esq.)

Lower Smith Street in the 1950s shows Acme Dry Goods, which later became a joke for popular Warner Brothers cartoons such as *Bugs Bunny* as a place to buy goods. The city of Perth Amboy was also mentioned in the movies *An American in Paris* and *A Canadian Yankee in King Arthur's Court*. In the contemporary image, the charm of the 1950s has been replaced by modern conveniences such as bargain stores and nail salons. (Historic image courtesy of Jack M. Dudas Esq.)

The Foodtown grocery store served many residents of Perth Amboy in its time as the site did in the past when it was a popular movie theater called the Strand in the 1940s. Those who shopped in Foodtown could see the structure where the screen once was. Now this site is a Rite Aid Pharmacy, providing residents with many services and conveniences. (Historic image courtesy of Barbara Booz.)

Shown is 1875 is Smith Street looking east from High Street before the great fire in November of that year. In the years to come, this served as a site for many businesses, including as H. L. Green, which was a five-and-dime store. In the mid-1970s, urban renewal transformed the area. Presently it is a residential area with townhomes that are both privately owned and owned by Raritan Bay Medical Center for its interns. (Historic image courtesy of Jack M. Dudas Esq.)

The Hotel Central, on Smith Street east of State Street, was ideally located in town. During the 1970s and 1980s, this hotel was replaced with a restaurant that former Perth Amboy High School students would remember as La Boue's, which was destroyed in a fire in the mid-1980s. This was replaced by Palmer Video, which went out of business in 1996. Presently the site serves as a Dunkin Donuts and a nail salon. (Historic image courtesy of Jack M. Dudas Esq.)

The Perth Amboy to Tottenville ferry was a gateway for many immigrants that came from Ellis Island to New Jersey. Many local factories employed these immigrants that settled into their own communities, such as Chicken Town, Little Budapest, and others. The ferry slip is no longer in use but serves as a reminder of the many immigrants that came to these shores. (Historic image courtesy of Jack M. Dudas Esq. and Barbara Booz.)

The Hotel Packer, known locally as the Packer Hotel or the Packer House, consisted of 100 rooms and 48 baths. The design was a European plan. Rates were $1.50 per day and up. Also located in the hotel was Lido Gardens, a Chinese restaurant renowned for its food (Above, courtesy of John K. Dyke and Barbara Booz; below, courtesy of Barbara Booz.)

On a cold winter night on March 17, 1969, a tragic fire destroyed the Hotel Packer and claimed several lives. The fire was caused by one of the residents smoking in bed. Now a senior housing facility that was built in the 1970s by the United Auto Workers (UAW) stands on the site. Many of the residents mention that they feel uneasy and claim the building is haunted, and they hear strange noises in the middle of the night. (Historic image courtesy of John K. Dyke.)

The Strand, seen here as it stood on lower Smith Street in June 1954, was one of seven theaters that occupied Perth Amboy during the 1950s. In 1928, the Strand and the Majestic Theater ushered in a new era for Perth Amboy theatergoers with a brand new sound system. The building was originally the George West Furniture Store. Presently it serves as a parklike area owned by Rite Aid Pharmacy. (Historic image courtesy of John K. Dyke and Barbara Booz.)

The Hotel Central, located on Smith Street, felt the blizzard of 1888 as did the rest of Perth Amboy. It wreaked havoc up and down the eastern seaboard to a degree that has never been equaled, with a total of a three-day accumulation of 20.9 inches. To this day, images of the blizzard of 1888 provide a romantic and historic significance in the minds of the today's youth. In contrast, the blizzard of 1996 caused some damage and shut down Smith Street for about four days. (Historic image courtesy of Dale Morris.)

Quinn's Store was a quaint little business located at 96 Smith Street that sold tea, coffee, and other dry goods. Subsequently, the building was demolished to make way for Roth Furniture. As time passed, this space was occupied by various businesses such as Dave's Army and Navy Store in the late 1980s. The present structure has gotten a face-lift as the home of Bargain Man, which utilizes all three floors of the building. (Historic image courtesy of the Perth Amboy Public Library.)

In the late 1960s or early 1970s, Mickey Finn's was the place to buy name-brand clothing for a fraction of the cost. This was due to slight imperfections in the clothing, such as a button missing or put on the wrong side or a label put upside down. Mickey Finn's closed in the mid-1980s. The building is still owned and maintained by the Lawrence lodge of the Independent Order of Odd Fellows. The thrift store Margaritas is the present tenant. (Historic image courtesy of Paul W. Wang.)

During the 1940s, five corners included the Watson Stock Exchange, which sat on the third floor of this magnificent architectural building. At the time, this intersection of Smith and State Streets was very congested and remains so today. People often use this site as a reference mark for giving directions. Presently the building serves as offices and houses a bank that has changed hands numerous times. (Historic image courtesy of Jack M. Dudas Esq. and Barbara Booz.)

TIMELESS AND CHANGING SMITH STREET

CHAPTER 2

OFF OF SMITH STREET

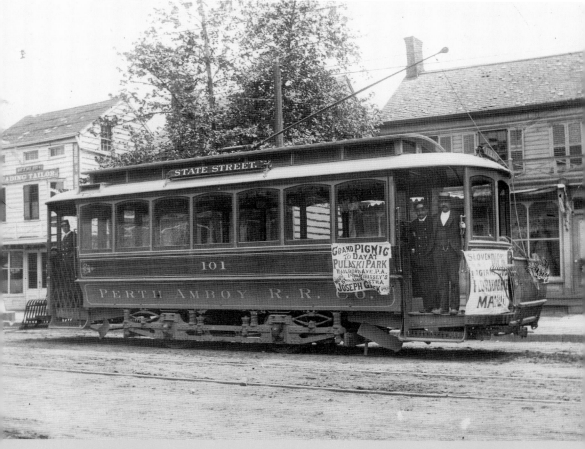

In the 1900s, the Perth Amboy trolley was the means of transportation for the average citizen. The Perth Amboy Transportation Company consisted of two types of cars—a summer and a winter car. The tracks went through Perth Amboy and up to New Brunswick Avenue, which was the turnaround point. The trolley depot was located on Upper Smith Street. (Courtesy of Jack M. Dudas Esq.)

The Masonic temple, located at 262 State Street, was built with funds raised by the Masonic fraternity in 1923 and 1924. The temple was managed by the Masonic Temple Building Society, which was made up of representatives elected by local lodges and the Raritan Craftsmen's Club.

Presently the building serves as a branch of Middlesex County Probation and Juvenile Justice. Recently it underwent renovations to make it more handicapped accessible. (Historic image courtesy of Jack M. Dudas Esq.)

Pictured around 1919, the building located at 308 State Street housed H. Levinston, a woman's hat shop with a lawyer's office upstairs. Presently Mi Tierra, a Spanish restaurant and bar, is located on the site with apartments above. With the increase of the city's population, any available space is utilized for residential housing. It is typical in Perth Amboy today for there to be housing above stores. (Historic image courtesy of Paul W. Wang.)

In 1927, the Majestic Theater, located on Madison Avenue, was the finest theater in Perth Amboy. It was a vaudeville theater and later a movie theater. In the late 1970s, it became an adult theater for a short time. After many petitions to save the building from demolition, the Second Baptist Church purchased the building, renovated it, and is presently utilizing it as a house of worship called the Cathedral. (Historic image courtesy of Jack M. Dudas Esq.)

First Street, as seen through the eyes of the residents during the blizzard of 1888, shows the damage of the storm. The photograph was taken on March 14, 1888. Transportation in Perth Amboy was brought to its knees. First Street, once hailed as a main thoroughfare in 1888, is no longer considered a main street. (Historic image courtesy of the Perth Amboy Public Library.)

Feiber and Shea's Bijou Theatre was mostly a vaudeville theater located on the corner of New Brunswick Avenue and Jefferson Street. A fire destroyed the building in 1913. In 1915, Frank Van Syckle purchased the property, and it became an automobile showroom that closed in the 1950s. It was then a storage area for many years that closed in 2006. After extensive remodeling, it houses several businesses. (Historic image courtesy of Barbara Booz.)

CHAPTER 3

BUSINESSES

The Perth Amboy Terra Cotta plant, located on Hall Avenue, opened in 1846 and was originally known as A. Hall and Sons. This company produced terra-cotta and porcelain. Hall Avenue was named in honor of Alfred Hall and his sons Edward and Eber. Later on, Edward became the mayor of Perth Amboy. (Courtesy of Paul W. Wang.)

George A. Seaman, pharmacist, was located on 283 High Street in 1863. In the mid–1930s, the pharmacy moved to 82 Smith Street where it served the public and many well–known faces such as Charlie White. Seaman's closed its doors to the public for the last time on November 19, 1998. The old location on High Street serves as the dentist office of Dr. Peter L. DeSciscio. (Historic image courtesy of Jack M. Dudas Esq.)

In the 1920s, King High Garage was one of many local garages in Perth Amboy. It was located on High Street until 2003 when it was relocated to outer State Street. Much of the King Street area was redeveloped into King Plaza, a high-rise apartment complex with stores on the first floor. These stores include Supremo Supermarket, which provides groceries within walking distance for tenants in the building. (Historic image courtesy of James Schreck, his son James Gougeon, and nephew, Robert Chryssikos.)

The Anchor Café, seen here in 1898 on the corner of New Brunswick Avenue and Prospect Street, served many pedestrians from the surrounding areas of Perth Amboy. The café presently located there, Karini II, still has the original copper ceiling that was installed during the late 1800s. This café is a must-see for anyone interested in architecture. The terra-cotta on this building was manufactured in the Perth Amboy Terra Cotta plant. (Historic image courtesy of Paul W. Wang.)

The Harbor Lights Tavern occupied the same location as Schantz and Eckert Machine Works. At one time the site was listed on the Coastal Heritage Trail. It was a popular gathering place for many of the residents of Perth Amboy and spawns fond memories. However, the tavern was destroyed by a fire in the 1980s. Many songs were written about the Harbor Lights Tavern. Presently the site is now the new sewage treatment sub-pumping station. (Historic image courtesy of Paul W. Wang.)

The Triangle Diner, as pictured in 1965, was named for its location where it sat on a triangular island between New Brunswick Avenue, Convery Boulevard, and Lawrie Street. Many residents enjoyed this typical 1950s diner. Outside of the diner directing traffic is police officer Artie Dyke. Kentucky Fried Chicken is presently located on the site. (Historic image courtesy of John K. Dyke.)

Opening day at Jefferson Market, located on New Brunswick Avenue, is pictured in 1909. Perth Amboy had a number of farmer's markets in the early 1900s. Due to easy access to roads and Raritan Bay, many farmers and merchants came to Jefferson Market to sell their goods. Presently the site houses the Laundry Factory and Quick Stop Deli. The other building on the site houses the Express Driving Academy. (Historic image courtesy of the Perth Amboy Public Library.)

Don's Bait and Tackle Stand was located on Front Street on the waterfront during the 1950s fishing season. This stand was very active. Due to pollution in the late 1970s, it was vacated and remained abandoned until the late 1980s when it was torn down in preparation for the new marina.

Presently the beautified waterfront is enjoyed by many city residents and visitors who use it for fishing, crabbing, walking, and many other outdoor recreational activities. (Historic image courtesy of Paul W. Wang.)

Seaboard Offices was located on Hall Avenue and Catherine Street and served as the offices for one of the largest known terra-cotta plants in New Jersey. Much of the terra-cotta work in New York City came from these factories in Perth Amboy. In the late 1990s, this location held the first Spanish woman-owned funeral parlor. Now on the site of the former terra-cotta plant is the Edward J. Patten Elementary School and the Ignacio Cruz Learning Center. (Historic image courtesy of Jack M. Dudas Esq.)

The Tea House was located on Front Street. Local beliefs were that the tea was stored here for safekeeping after the Boston Tea Party, but it was in fact built by Matthias Bruen in the 1820s as a warehouse. Bruen was a partner of the great tea merchant William H. Smith of New York, thus it was called the Tea House. It was demolished in the early 1950s for the Harbor Terrace complex and was located where the parking lot is now. (Historic image courtesy of John K. Dyke and Barbara Booz.)

Schantz and Eckert Machine Works, pictured about 1906, was founded in 1884 and situated on the waterfront. It repaired marine engines as well as general machinery. The company built some of the machinery for the *Holland,* the first U.S. submarine, and fashioned parts for Dr. Solomon Andrews's famous dirigible. The company closed in the 1940s. Presently the site is included in the redevelopment of the waterfront. (Historic image courtesy of the Perth Amboy Public Library.)

Pictured around 1908, Patrick Convery Groceries and Ship Chandlery was located at what was considered lower High Street at the time and served the public and the surrounding area's merchants with goods and groceries to maintain their vessels. The chandlery also bought and sold oysters, an industry that Perth Amboy was famous for. It was extensively remodeled and is now privately owned. (Historic image courtesy of the Perth Amboy Public Library.)

The Perth Amboy Dry Dock Company was founded in 1887 by John Runyon. Located at the foot of Broad Street, it built tugboats, car floats, and barges. In 1918, it was purchased by the Raritan Dry Dock Company and doubled in size. After the 1930s, the company repaired large ships. The company closed its Perth Amboy location in the 1990s. Presently the site is slated for urban renewal. (Historic image courtesy of the Perth Amboy Public Library.)

During the early 1800s, the waterfront area was the center of business. Warehouses and stores with domestic and imported goods gave way to outdoor markets. Farmer's markets were constructed to provide an orderly supply of goods to the urban residents of the city. By the late 1950s, the Perth Amboy markets had lost too many customers and closed. In their place stands State-Fayette Gardens, an apartment complex that boasted to be the most modern apartment development in Perth Amboy in its time. (Historic image courtesy of Paul W. Wang.)

The Copperworks was located on Elm Street from the early 1900s to the late 1960s. It was so named because it used to smelt copper ore. Due to the decline in industry in Perth Amboy in the mid-1970s, the Copperworks was sold to the Raritan Steel Company, which built a new processing plant, shown here under construction. Raritan Steel was sold in the early 1990s to Co-Steel, which in turn sold it to Gerdau Steel, the present owner. (Historic image courtesy of Jack M. Dudas Esq.)

On July 9, 1980, tragedy struck Perth Amboy. Many businesses were lost due to a major fire known as the Cableworks fire that lasted for three days. The fire was believed to be caused by a spark that was near cleaning solvents. Many fire departments were called in to put out the blaze. For many years, the site was left a shell, but recently the remaining structures were torn down. Now the site is a vacant lot. (Historic image courtesy of Paul W. Wang.)

Fertig's Department Store is a fourth-generation family owned and run business in Perth Amboy. Fertig Hosiery was established in 1919. In 1960, the family purchased the adjacent building to expand their business. Presently the company services the city's parochial and public schools, city workers, and the local hospitals by providing uniforms. It is one of the oldest businesses in Perth Amboy that is still in existence besides Finks Department Store. (Historic image courtesy of the Fertig family.)

Sciortino's Pizzeria is a fourth-generation family owned and run business. It was established at 397 New Brunswick Avenue in 1932. The pizzeria was forced to close in July 2003 due to urban renewal. It reopened in South Amboy in May 2004 and is located on 132 South Broadway Avenue. Sciortino's boasts to be the fifth pizzeria in New Jersey and the ninth in the United States. On its old site in Perth Amboy, the new municipal complex now stands. (Historic image courtesy of the Paulo and Francis Sciortino and Lou Seminski Sr..)

INSTITUTIONS

A well-known institution in Perth Amboy is the Great Bed Lighthouse. Known as the Amboy beacon, this lighthouse has been serving ships that come to Raritan Bay for many years. Once manned, it is now automated and maintained by the U.S. Coast Guard. (Courtesy of Paul W. Wang.)

The Perth Amboy train station was located between Market and Smith Streets in the 1920s. The train station building was purchased and moved, and still stands on Lewis Street as a private residence. In 1923, a new railroad station was built with lower train tracks. Presently, through a grant from former New Jersey governor Christine Todd Whitman and Senator Frank R. Lautenberg, it was remodeled, and the result is what modern-day residents know and use. (Historic image courtesy of the Perth Amboy Public Library.)

The William C. McGinnis School was built in 1899. Formerly the Perth Amboy High School, this collegiate-looking building of neo-Jacobean design stands on the site of Perth Amboy's 17th-century town burial ground. The removal of its famous walls of ivy and the installation of metal sash has considerably changed the building's appearance. During the 1990s, an outer glass-enclosed stairwell was added to the building. (Historic image courtesy of the Perth Amboy Public Library.)

The city hall was built in 1766. The north wing was added in 1909, and it remained unaltered until 1870 when the mansard roof was added. The building has been used over the years as a town house, a court, a school, and the police station. It is still one of the oldest working city hall buildings in the state of New Jersey. (Historic image courtesy of the Perth Amboy Public Library.)

Pictured in the 1930s, Protection Hook and Ladder Company Engine No. 1 and Lincoln Hose Company No. 1 were located on State Street next to the former high school, which is now the William C. McGinnis School. The building was demolished in early 1960s and the companies moved to High Street. The site now serves as a parking lot for the school and some of the stores next to it. (Historic image courtesy of the Perth Amboy Public Library.)

The First Presbyterian Church was built in 1802 and is the second-oldest parish in Perth Amboy. The first minister was David Simpson, the chaplain of the *Henry and Francis*, a ship transporting Scottish refugees to Raritan Bay. Known for its Gothic design, the parish was built by A. F. Leicht, a New York architect who designed churches for several New Jersey cities. It is still in use today with an active membership. (Historic image courtesy of the Perth Amboy Public Library.)

The Grace English Lutheran Church on Jefferson Street opposite the public library was built in 1903. Though considered a temporary chapel when it was erected, it served the congregation for a half century until it was replaced in 1958 with the brick Gothic contemporary edifice that stands today at 600 New Brunswick Avenue. The original site now serves as a parking lot for local stores. (Historic image courtesy of the Perth Amboy Public Library.)

St. Mary's School, located at 103 Center Street, was built in 1882. It served both as a school and as a convent. The original school was built on the grounds of the present church rectory in a wooden building that was 25 feet tall and cost $400. The building is Victorian Renaissance Revival, featuring polychrome brickwork and fine terra-cotta designs. Presently the building serves as office space for Catholic Charities. (Historic image courtesy of the Perth Amboy Public Library.)

St. Mary's Roman Catholic Church was founded in 1844 by Irish immigrants. The structure was built between 1903 and 1905 and is one of the oldest Catholic parishes in New Jersey. During a severe electrical storm in 2003, lightning hit the church tower, and one of the spires fell into the building, causing severe damage. The spires were subsequently removed from the building. The church still has an active membership. (Historic image courtesy of the Perth Amboy Public Library.)

St. Peter's Episcopal Church was founded in 1698 and is the oldest church in Perth Amboy. The churchyard was constructed in 1722, and the church structure was built in 1852. Several tombstones bear damage from cannon fire during the Revolutionary War. The cemetery is the final resting place for Thomas Mundy Peterson, the first black voter in the United States, as well as many other famous local citizens, including James Kearny Smith. (Historic image courtesy of the Perth Amboy Public Library.)

The Congregation of Beth Israel Synagogue purchased the Wesley Methodist Church at Madison Avenue and Jefferson Street on September 10, 1960, at 1:00 p.m. Growing in numbers, the congregation found itself in need of larger facilities and moved to Scotch Plains. Since the congregation left, the building has housed many different of religions. Presently it is the Victory and Triumph Worship Center. (Historic image courtesy of Paul W. Wang.)

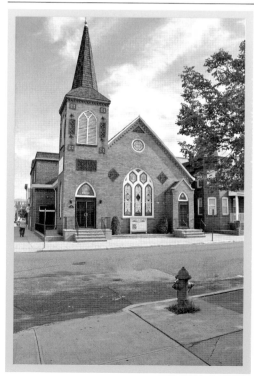

Founded in 1866, the Simpson Methodist Church is grand in scale, yet it has simplicity of design that makes it one of Perth Amboy's most imposing religious edifices. When the town clock was installed in the flat-topped Italianate tower in 1869, it was already the tallest structure in the city. The worship room is entirely sheathed with cedar and other woods. It is still in use today and has an active membership. (Historic image courtesy of the Simpson Methodist Church.)

The federal building was under construction, as seen on November 2, 1904. It was located on Jefferson Street and opened its doors April 2, 1906. It was demolished to make way for the present-day post office that opened its doors on April 14, 1937. The new building prides itself as a Spanish colonial with a terra-cotta trim that has been glazed to have a brown luster to it. The building is still used to this day and prides itself of its art deco interior. (Historic image courtesy of Paul W. Wang.)

The U.S. Customs House on Jefferson Street, pictured here in 1903, was founded in 1884 and used as offices for government officials who processed paperwork and collected duty for the import and export of goods into and out of the country. It closed its doors in the late 1920s. Customs houses were typically located in a seaport or in a city on a major river with access to the ocean like Perth Amboy. On the site now is a parking lot. (Historic image courtesy of Jack M. Dudas Esq.)

School No. 4 was built in 1896; a brand new building on the corner of Smith and Stockton Streets. The building was an 11-room edifice with three stories and a cupola. In 1902, the janitor requested "that steps be taken to keep the cows and geese off the finely kept lawn." High school classes were held in there until 1900. The building was demolished to make way for the Dr. Herbert N. Richardson School. (Historic image courtesy of the Perth Amboy Public Library.)

From the early 1960s through the 1970s, Friday night on Smith Street was known as "cruise night." Many youths formed a caravan of cars that they drove up and down Smith Street. They did this for many hours each Friday until the 1970s when the local police believed cruise night was a nuisance and banned it. Many store residents felt they lost business do to the enforcement of this law. Today cruise night is just a pleasant memory for many residents. (Historic image courtesy of Paul W. Wang.)

INSTITUTIONS

Standing proudly on display in city hall circle in the 1930s is one of Perth Amboy's newest traffic safety vehicles. This state-of-the-art vehicle was equipped with loudspeakers to help to maintain traffic at fire and crime scenes and prevent accidents when traffic lights were out. They also educated the youth on safety of crossing the streets. Presently the traffic safety department has not change much, except, of course, they use modern vehicles. (Historic image courtesy of Jack M. Dudas Esq.)

The East Jersey Men's Club was believed to be located on Front Street and was built in 1684. This structure was demolished and several other structures were put up. The last private home was destroyed in 2007 in a fire. The structure has been torn down, and the property was up for sale by its owner in 2008. (Historic image courtesy of the Perth Amboy Public Library.)

CHAPTER 5

ALONG THE
WATERFRONT

An aerial photograph of Water Street from August 11, 1936, shows a pleasant summer day on the shores of Perth Amboy. Many visitors came to the city to do their shopping and enjoyed the beaches and the relaxing, clear waters of the Raritan Bay. (Courtesy of Jack M. Dudas Esq.)

PERTH AMBOY

69

Front Street in the 1920s was mainly an industrial area because of its ideal location near the water. Today industrial businesses are being replaced by residential homes and commercial businesses catering to the public, such as the Maid of Perth Collectible store, the Barge Restaurant, and the Armory Restaurant. Many residents enjoy leisurely walks along the new piers and docks on Perth Amboy's waterfront. (Historic image courtesy of Jack M. Dudas Esq.)

Pictured on July 25, 1941, Perth Amboy's south shore waterfront was where warm summer breezes of Raritan Bay made Perth Amboy beaches popular. They were popular during World War II for numerous economic reasons, such as saving on gasoline and rubber that were necessary for the war effort. Due to pollution, the water is presently unfit for swimming. (Historic image courtesy of Jack M. Dudas Esq.)

South Shore Bathing Beaches - July 25, 1941.

The Raritan Yacht Club went through three different structural changes due to fires. The last fire took place in 1915. The present-day structure was built in 1919 and remains the same today except for some changes that reflect the times, such as new docks and a new rear balcony. The surrounding homes in the area were built up over time. (Historic image courtesy of Jack M. Dudas Esq. and Barbara Booz.)

Seen in the 1960s, the Gulf fueling station and hot dog stand was vacated in the late 1970s and remained abandoned until the late 1980s when it was torn down to in preparation for the new marina. Presently, the newly renovated waterfront is enjoyed by many local residents, some of whom own boats and utilize the harbor slips. (Historic image courtesy of John K. Dyke and Barbara Booz.)

During the 1930s, these courts hosted many known tennis professionals who participated in tournaments and offered lessons to the residents, and they were widely used by the public. Today the site serves as a location for after school programs for children sponsored by the police department. The buildings and courts have deteriorated due to lack of interest. The clay courts have been replaced by black top. (Historic image courtesy of Jack M. Dudas Esq.)

The lower Sadowsky Parkway was under construction during the 1930s. These clay courts were used for tennis as well as for an ice-skating rink until the 1970s when they were black topped over. The clay courts served the public for many years and were very popular in the 1930s. Back then, one was lucky to get to use these famous clay courts. Presently, the courts are still used by residents but are not as popular. (Historic image courtesy of the Perth Amboy Public Library.)

During the early 1800s, the waterfront was the center of business, with eateries, boardinghouses, and waterfront hotels, which were located on Front and lower Smith Streets. Two of the best-known hotels were Hartmann's Hotel and the Ferry Hotel. These hotels were crowded in the summer with vacationers from New Jersey and New York who came to enjoy the salty air and the waters of the Arthur Kill. These hotels were demolished in the early 1930s to make way for Bayview Park. (Historic image courtesy of the Perth Amboy Public Library.)

SUMMER FUN IN THE PARKS

A relaxing game of shuffleboard in Caledonia Park in the 1930s was a popular activity for Perth Amboy's residents. They had competitions with prize trophies. Many people also came to this park for relaxation, the salty air of the bay, and Sunday afternoon picnics. (Courtesy of the Perth Amboy Public Library.)

Caledonia Park, as seen in 1936, was named for the ship bound to Perth Amboy from Scotland. The park was known for cherry trees and many other grand old trees and, in its time, shuffleboard. The park is an ideal location for pleasant Sunday afternoon relaxation and a walk on the waterfront. Recently this park went under renovation and is utilized as a playground for children. (Historic image courtesy of the Perth Amboy Public Library.)

Roessler's Gymnasium was built in 1911 and combined the functions of a private gymnasium with those of a stable and coach house. In the 1930s, it held theatrical shows and athletic events that were open to the public for many years. After the gymnasium was left to the city, it rapidly began to deteriorate. By the early 1990s, the gymnasium was demolished for the renovation of Caledonia Park and is utilized as a playground for children. (Historic image courtesy of Paul W. Wang.)

Bayview Park, seen here in November 1936 when it was first constructed, gives the residents a magnificent view of Raritan Bay. In the 1980s, Concerts by the Bay was instituted, which offers a relaxing mix of popular and classical music to enjoy on warm Sunday afternoons. The park was remodeled in 2007, offering residents a new gazebo to enjoy. (Historic image courtesy of the Perth Amboy Public Library.)

The statue of George Washington was presented in 1896 and erected by local Danish sculptor Nels Alling. It was a gift from the Danish people of Perth Amboy. The circle was remodeled in 1983, and an arch was built to commemorate the city's tercentennial. Commemorative certificates were sold to raise money for the building of this arch. Market Square Park remains a popular area for residents to take leisurely strolls. (Historic image courtesy of Jack M. Dudas Esq.)

Washington Park, as seen in January 1930, is located on outer New Brunswick Avenue and was built as a part of the Works Progress Administration (WPA) program. It has served youth from the 1930s to present. The park improved over a period of time, when swings, a cement pond, and a ball field were constructed and enjoyed by many of the residents of Perth Amboy. (Historic image courtesy of the Perth Amboy Public Library.)

Time went by, and Washington Park was developed. It housed a cement wading pool where the youth of Perth Amboy cooled off on hot summer days. Water sprayed from a central obelisk into the pool. As time progressed, the wading pool was not used, and due to lack of interest, it was forced to be closed and was replaced by a playground. (Historic image courtesy of the Perth Amboy Public Library.)

Albert G. Waters Stadium was constructed around 1929 and is located on Eagle Avenue. It suffered a fire in the late 1970s that caused major damage and forced it to be rebuilt. Recently it was renovated again. It is used today by Perth Amboy High School to hold many of its athletic events and graduations. Many residents enjoy the facility as well. (Historic image courtesy of the Perth Amboy Public Library.)

CHAPTER 7

HOMES

Parker Castle was once a majestic home in Perth Amboy for the Parker family. This once-proud estate hosted magnificent parties. By the late 1940s or early 1950s, this home was in ruins. Notice the broken windows and neglect of the majestic garden fences due to lack of care. (Courtesy of the Perth Amboy Public Library.)

85

The Dublin Lighthouse is seen here in 1903 on the corner of New Brunswick Avenue and Prospect Street. It was used as a home for the men that staffed the Great Beds Lighthouse. The service became automated in the late 1930s, and the staff was no longer needed. The home was abandoned and began to deteriorate. It was destroyed by the city in the 1940s, and a small factory was built. For the last 35 years, this site served as a body shop for repairing cars. (Historic image courtesy of the Perth Amboy Public Library.)

Perth Amboy's waterfront in the area of Water Street is considered to be the bluff. Many residents thought of the bluff as the "residential streets of choice" where expensive Victorian homes lined both sides. At one time, residents of the bluff had a private beach. Many influential families had homes along the bluff. Little has changed on the bluff, except now there is an apartment complex consisting of one building that was built in the fall of 1948. (Historic image courtesy of the Perth Amboy Public Library.)

RESIDENCES ON THE BLUFF.

Parker Castle was built in 1670 by the Parker family, wealthy owners of a commercial fleet. In 1760, Capt. James Parker added a section made of wood that was so large the building became known as Parker Castle. The family hosted many elaborate affairs on their magnificent grounds, such as balls, card parties, theatrical shows, and athletic events. The home was torn down in the 1950s, and the site remained unoccupied until the 1980s. Modern-day condominiums now stand on the site. (Historic image courtesy of the Perth Amboy Public Library.)

The Proprietary House is located at 149 Kearny Avenue. It was built between 1762 and 1764 by English master builder John Edward Pryor and remodeled in 1809. It served as the home of William Franklin, the last royal governor of New Jersey. The property was known under three names: the Governor's Mansion, the Proprietary House, and the Westminster. Presently it is serving as a museum that is open to the public and run by the Proprietary House Organization. (Historic image courtesy of Jack M. Dudas Esq.)

Here is the Kearny Cottage around 1918. It was built in 1781 by Michael Kearny and served as the home of the Kearny family, including Commodore Lawrence Kearny, who opened up trade with China. It was originally located on High Street but was moved several times. During the 1950s, its final resting place became 63 Catalpa Avenue. It serves as a historical museum open for tours to the public and is run by the Kearny Cottage Historical Association. (Historic image courtesy of Paul W. Wang.)

The Gov. Morgan F. Larson house, located on 225 High Street, was the home of the first proprietary governor. The original structure on the site was built in 1684 and demolished before the American Revolution. That structure was replaced by another privately owned home, which was demolished in the 1920s to make way for Larson's house. Today the house remains privately owned. (Historic image courtesy of the Perth Amboy Public Library.)

The Thomas Bartow house is located at 235 Water Street. It was built in 1730 as the home of a prominent early citizen and is considered the oldest house in Perth Amboy. Playwright and historian William Dunlap (1766–1839) received his early education at this house. It was moved from Market Square in 1923 to make way for the First Baptist Church. Now the house is privately owned. (Historic image courtesy of Dale Morris.)

The Franz Roessler house, on the corner of High and Lewis Streets, was built in 1890. The many gables, varied surface treatment, turned corner posts, and irregular window design of this sprawling frame house is typical of the late Victorian taste for eclectic forms and decoration. According to local beliefs, this house was a speakeasy and house of ill repute in the 1920s. Today the house remains unoccupied. (Historic image courtesy of Paul W. Wang.)

The W. M. H. McCormick house is located at 225 High Street. Built in 1892, this house is in the Queen Anne style with basic asymmetry and contrasting materials. Its tight massing shows evidence of the emerging Colonial Revival style. William McCormick was a physician. His daughter Rose McCormick was a teacher at Perth Amboy High School and founded the Perth Amboy's Woman's Club. Presently the house remains occupied and still maintains its original glory. (Historic image courtesy of the Perth Amboy Public Library.)

Willocks Lane is where the earliest houses were built by the East Jersey Proprietors to bring in settlers, such as baker James Wait. The area was redeveloped during the late 1940s and early 1950s to make way for Harbor Terrace, a building complex that offered luxury apartments varying is sizes from studios to two bedrooms. Changes like Harbor Terrace insure many "nows" in Perth Amboy's future. (Historic image courtesy of John K. Dyke and Barbara Booz.)

ACROSS AMERICA, PEOPLE ARE DISCOVERING SOMETHING WONDERFUL. *THEIR HERITAGE.*

Arcadia Publishing is the leading local history publisher in the United States. With more than 3,000 titles in print and hundreds of new titles released every year, Arcadia has extensive specialized experience chronicling the history of communities and celebrating America's hidden stories, bringing to life the people, places, and events from the past. To discover the history of other communities across the nation, please visit:

www.arcadiapublishing.com

Customized search tools allow you to find regional history books about the town where you grew up, the cities where your friends and family live, the town where your parents met, or even that retirement spot you've been dreaming about.